THIS BOOK BELONGS TO

PHONE:

EMAIL:

START DATE:

END DATE:

EMERGENCY CONTACT

NAME:

PHONE:

RELATIONSHIP: